the hammer and other poems
o martelo e outros poemas

Adelaide Ivánova

the hammer and other poems

o martelo e outros poemas

Translated from Brazilian Portuguese by
Rachel Long and Francisco Vilhena

poetry translation centre

First published in 2019
by the Poetry Translation Centre Ltd
The Albany, Douglas Way, London, SE8 4AG

www.poetrytranslation.org

The Brazilian Portuguese poems in this selection first appeared in *o martelo* (douda correria; 2016)

The Portuguese translation of the Paul Celan quote on p24 is taken from Flávio R. Kothe's *Paul Celan - Poemas* (Tempo Brasileiro; 1977). The English translation on p25 is taken from Michael Hamburger's *The Poems of Paul Celan* (Anvil; 1988)

ISBN: 978-0-9575511-2-1

A catalogue record for this book is available from the British Library

Typeset in Minion by Poetry Translation Centre Ltd

Series Editor: Edward Doegar
Cover Design: Kit Humphrey
Printed in the UK by T.J. International

Obra publicada com apoio do Ministério das Relações Exteriores do Brasil em cooperação com a Fundação Biblioteca Nacional / Ministério da Cidadania.

Work published with the support of the Ministry of Foreign Affairs of Brazil in cooperation with the National Library Foundation / Ministry of Citizenship.

The PTC is supported using public funding by Arts Council England

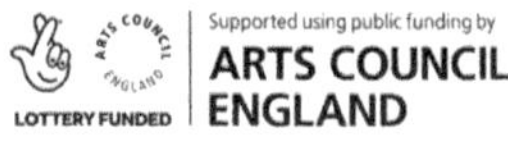

FUNDAÇÃO BIBLIOTECA NACIONAL
MINISTÉRIO DA CIDADANIA
MINISTÉRIO DAS RELAÇÕES EXTERIORES

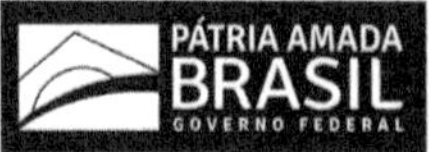

Contents

Introduction

Adelaide Ivánova was born in Recife, Brazil in 1982. A poet, journalist, photographer, activist and performance artist, she currently lives between Berlin and Cologne. She is the author of the collections *13 Nudes* and *o martelo* (*the hammer*), the latter awarded the 2018 Rio de Janeiro Literature Prize for Poetry. Adelaide's work has been featured in several anthologies, and has been translated into Galician, German, Greek, Italian and Spanish. She curates the anarcho-feminist zine of queer and erotic poetry *MAIS PORNÔ, PFVR!* (*MORE PORN, PLS!*), and is a co-founder of the feminist collective RESPEITA! (RESPECT!), a coalition of Brazilian female poets. She has also published several photobooks, including *Autotomy*, a photographic study of two trans teenagers living in Berlin and *Adelaide*, an ongoing project that documents the daily routine of her grandmother.

This book contains a selection of poems from *o martelo*. Published in 2016, *o martelo* is divided in two parts, both told in the voice of the same woman, first as a rape victim and then as an adulteress. This presentation is inspired by Constantine the Great, the first Christian emperor, who viewed rape victims and women who committed adultery as criminals and therefore subject to corporal punishment. With *o martelo*, Adelaide attempts to build a narrative that considers the body and the woman in the aftermath. There is tension and hurt, and a need to fight back, to be unsilenced, deal with the unresolved and take over, 'i sleep with a hammer / under my pillow / in case someone walks in again' ('the hammer').

With a background in journalism and documentary photography, there is a sense of how non-fiction informs her writing – Adelaide's poetics come in the form of reports, assessments, vignette-like explorations of trauma and emotional turmoil. There is a clinical procedural quality to it, an almost forensic-like reconstruction of womanhood, 'it / will all return to normal / i can't believe it but it seems / to make sense' ('the dog').

Adelaide's work is subversive, caustic, cynical and agitating in a way that is also disconcertingly casual:

> people drink so they can die
> without dying much
> she asks why didn't i
> scream seeing as i hadn't been
> gagged i didn't respond but i know
> that you are born with the gag on

Permeated with subtle references that range from classical Roman mythology to folklore of the Brazilian northeast, Adelaide's work is of a poet animating her own tradition, one in which she borrows and takes and molds and subverts, one in which Hilda Hilst, essential twentieth-century Brazilian author provocateur, can be found in the voice of one of Adelaide's mules, 'i can even hear the stones and their misfortune' ('the mule'), alongside Lavinia, Thalia and Philomela.

Adelaide talks back to a tradition and reshapes it. From the beautiful playful praxis of the work of concrete poet João Cabral de Melo Neto, 'i saw joão maravilha / stone cabral // . . . poetics / syllables / sonido / rhythm' ('el martillo'), comes an admiration for shape and form and sound ever so present in 1950s Brazil and onwards, one which transpired into other media, such as the paintings of Lygia Clark and Hélio Oiticica or the music of Chico Buarque. In Angélica Freitas she finds the virtues of sadness and humour, the vitriol of cynicism, of never letting up, never surrendering.

For example, take Angélica's poem 'woman is a construct' and Adelaide's 'the married woman', two beautiful forceful eruptions of badassery:

woman is a construct
she must be

woman is basically meant
to be a residential complex
all the same
all plastered over
just in different colors

i in particular am a woman
with exposed bricks
at social gatherings i tend to be
the worst dressed

i sit in a circle
according
to the event
i swallow
the wine
i deposit
olive
pits on
the corner
i control
the fertile period
i pretend
to be registered
vaccinated
beautiful

Adelaide's poetry inhabits the transformative power of being a woman, and plays with the possibility of that power as weapon; a sense of nonconformity is ever-present, its war cry turned words out of wombs, limbs, mouths, 'guilty is the woman' ('the sentence'). Drawing inspiration from Susan Sontag's study of representations of pain, the aim is 'not to evoke but to show'. It comes in waves, rippling alongside a palpable sense of irony, object of defiance.

There are several echoes in her work, like pellets in a shotgun, always at the ready: Adília Lopes the silent contemplator, Matilde Campilho wunderkind of the heartstrings, Ricardo Reis the quiet Pessoa heteronym, and Anne Sexton, Sylvia Plath, Emily Dickinson, Lady Gaga, Marguerite Yourcenar. It is a vast landscape. And of course there is *cordel* and *brega* and *frevo* and *boi*, Chico Science, Dilma Rousseff, Luiz Inácio Lula da Silva, Maria Bonita, Vinicius de Moraes, Maria Felipa, Paulo Leminski, Ana Cristina César, Armando Freitas Filho, Cássia Eller, Caio Fernando Abreu, Adélia Prado, Manuel Bandeira, Recife, Pernambuco, Berlin. I could go on.

Then comes the hammer, ultimate weapon, precursor of resistance, 'optimal object / for good sleeping / or hitting nails on the head' ('the hammer'). These incisive and at times surreal poems claw open the body and its politics. Hammer on.

Francisco Vilhena

Poems

o martelo

o papa quando morre
leva uma
marteladinha
na testa eu nunca
martelei
ninguém
nem papa nem príncipe nem rei
quando a procissão
tem que seguir
o capataz dá três
marteladas
no andor e os
costaleiros seguem
martelo
é um decassílabo heroico
com tônicas nas posições
três seis e dez quando
o atleta termina o
molinete três voltinhas
em torno de si mesmo
pode lançar o
martelo
que pesa sete kilos
duzentos e sessenta gramas
marx nunca falou sobre
martelo
algum quem já viu
escola de pensamento ter

the hammer

whenever the pope dies
he gets
a little blow with a hammer
on his forehead i never
hammered
anyone
not a pope or a prince or a king
whenever the procession
has to go on
the overseer hits
the hammer
three times
on the stand
and the followers follow
hammer
is a heroic decasyllable
with tonics on the positions
three six and ten when
the athlete finishes the
rotation three spins
over his own axis
he can release
the hammer
weighing seven kilos
two hundred and seventy grams
marx never said anything about any
hammer
has anyone ever seen

símbolo qual seria o símbolo
da escola de frankfurt se
adorno tivesse escolhido um?
quando thor bate seu
martelo
é sinal de chuva e trovão
mas é a flor do mandacaru
que anuncia chuva no
sertão para o tubarão-martelo o
martelo
funciona como uma asa
estabilizando seus
movimentos além disso
o ritual de acasalamento
dos tubarões-martelo
é muito violento
na bandeira da albânia
comunista substituíram o
martelo
por um fuzil o
martelo
é um objeto ótimo
que serve pra dormir bem
ou pregar pregos.

any school of thought having
a symbol what would the symbol
of the frankfurt school be had
adorno picked one?
when thor strikes his
hammer
it signals rain and thunder
but it's the flower of the mandacaru
that announces rain in
the sertão for the hammerhead shark the
hammer
works as a wing
stabilising his
movements and also
the mating ritual
of hammerhead sharks
is incredibly violent
in communist
albania they replaced the
hammer
with a rifle the
hammer
is an optimal object
for good sleeping
or hitting nails on the head.

a sentença

duas releituras de duas odes de ricardo reis

I

pesa o decreto atroz, o fim certeiro.
pesa a sentença igual do juiz iníquo.
pesa como bigorna em minhas costas:
    um homem foi hoje absolvido.

se a justiça é cega, só o xampu é neutro:
quão pouca diferença na inocência
do homem e das hienas. deixem-me em paz!
    antes encham-me de vinho

a taça, qu'inda que bem ruim me deixe
ébria, console-me a alcoólica amnésia
e olvide o que de fato é tal sentença:
    a mulher é a culpada.

the sentence

two re-readings of two odes by ricardo reis

I

the atrocious decree weighs, the certain ending.
the equitable sentence of the iniquitous judge weighs.
weighs like an anvil on my back:
    a man was absolved today.

if justice is blind, only shampoo is neutral:
such little difference in the innocence
of the man and of the hyenas. leave me alone!
    rather fill me with wine

the cup, even though awful might leave me
drunk, console me alcoholic amnesia
and forget what is in fact the sentence:
    guilty is the woman.

II

pese do fiel juiz igual sentença
em cada pobre homem, que não há motivo
para tanto. não fiz mal nenhum à mulher e
    foi grande meu espanto

quando ela se ofendeu. exagerada, agora
reclama, fez denúncia e drama, mas na hora
nem se mexeu. culpa é dela: encheu à brava
    a garbosa cara.

se a justiça é cega, só a topeira é sábia.
celebro abonançado o evidente indulto
pois sou apenas homem, não um monstro! leixai
    à mulher o trauma.

II

weigh the faithful judge's equitable sentence
in every poor man, there is no need
for that. i did not hurt the woman and
look at my surprise

when she found herself offended. exaggerating, now
she claims she complained and oh the drama! but back then
she didn't even move. it's her fault: she stuffed her
drunken face.

if justice is blind, only the mole is wise
i welcome the relaxed and obvious pardon
as i am only a man, not a monster! bequeath
the trauma to the woman.

os testículos

em alemão visor de porta
é espião olho mágico em
português *peephole* é o
que se diz no paquistão
cuja língua oficial é o
inglês judas é a palavra
em francês aproximando
vigilância da traição
o que me parece fruto
de resignada sensatez

as testemunhas não são
traças não viram nada como
as traças mas defendem
com histeria a inocência do
príncipe usando-me a mim
como medida como podem
ser chamadas de testemunhas
testemunhas que lá não estavam

antes não se faziam as coisas
por medo da guilhotina hoje
apenas pelo medo de ser
pego no flagra

(no paquistão se a vítima
não encontrar quatro testemunhas
oculares é ela que será
processada na inglaterra do
século 18 se a vítima não

the testicles

in german peephole
is spy magic eye in
portuguese peephole is
what is said in pakistan
whose official language is
english judas is the word
in french approximating
vigilance to treason
which seems to me a fruit
of wise resignation

witnesses are not
moths they did not see a thing like
moths do but they defend
hysterically the innocence of
the prince using me
as measure how can
they be called witnesses
witnesses who weren't there

in the old days you wouldn't do things
out of fear of the guillotine today
merely for fear of being
caught in the act

(in pakistan if the victim
is unable to find four eye
witnesses she is the one being
prosecuted in 18th century
england if the victim had

tivesse gritado e se debatido
se estabelecia que a denúncia
não valia)

as testemunhas inventaram
parentescos amizades citaram
relações imaginárias um padrasto
que fui ter com o príncipe
em seu quarto está tudo nos autos
palavras tantas entram em
mítica instância viram
documento poema oficial
mas incompetente as testemunhas
todas sabem que mentem o que elas
não sabem é que em latim
testemunhas e testículos
advêm da mesma base o que nesse
caso é um insulto com os testículos
essa coisa tão maravilhosa
que são os testículos
testis é o nome em latim
de onde dizem se inspirou
valéry para dar ao *monsieur*
o nome de *teste* que Humboldt
me mandou ler e como Humboldt
tem belos testículos faço tudo
que ele pede as testemunhas
todas mentem não dizem nada
com nada e se consideram
estupro sexo é porque não
fazem ideia como eu faço
do que é uma bela trepada.

not screamed and resisted
it would be established that the complaint
was invalid)

the witnesses invented
parental affiliations friendships quoted
imaginary relationships a stepfather
that i went to see with the prince
in his room it's all in the deed
many words going into
mythical instance turning
document official poem
but incompetent and the witnesses
all know they lie what they
don't know is that in latin
witness and testicle
share the same root which in this
case is an insult to the testicles
and the wonderful thing
that testicles are
testis is the latin name
which people say inspired
valéry to give monsieur
the name of *teste* and as Humboldt
has beautiful testicles i'll do anything
he asks the witnesses
all lie what they say doesn't make
any sense and if they think of
rape as sex it's because they have
no idea like i do of
what a good fuck is.

a mula

> um silêncio amamentado com veneno,
> um silêncio imenso
> – *Paul Celan, tradução de Flávio R. Kothe*

mede o valor de seu empenho
e afirmações tendo
como medida o peso que carrega
como boa mula não faz ideia
de quem a monta mas
está a seu serviço

como toda boa mula
empaca na beira do
abismo não morrer
é sua vingança
filomena sem língua
e mula
não pula por ódio
não por esperança
(e nisso há uma diferença
fundamental).

a mula-lavínia
também teve sua língua
arrancada de lucrécia
mula e adormecida
não arrancaram
nada mas a chantagem
é também uma mordaça

the mule

put a silence over it,
stilled with poison, great
– *Paul Celan, translated by Michael Hamburger*

measures the worth of her effort
and affirms by having
as measure the weight she carries
like a good mule she has no idea
who is riding her but
she is at their service

like every good mule
she halts by the edge of
the cliff not dying
is her vengeance
tongueless philomela
and mule
does not jump for hatred
nor for hope
(and in it there is a fundamental
difference).

mule-lavínia
also had her tongue
pulled out from lucrécia
mule and sleeping
they didn't pull anything
out but blackmail
is also a gag

a mula-talia também
dormia quando foi
violada
foi maury e mula
que conseguiu
abrir a boca
e ao virar asno
mudou o próprio
nome e o das coisas
a nova mula aprendeu
alemão e *vergewaltigung*
deixa de ser o que é
vira um som qualquer
dito com a mesma
entonação que cometa
fúria jacaré passarinho
fósforo procissão pedra
cacto

a mula empacada
quase muda ao menos
nunca foi surda
'até das pedras lhes ouço a desventura'
cada um tem o que diz
a mula em zarathustra
a mula de hilst
mas o rouxinol que canta
é o rouxinol macho.

mule-talia also
slept when she was
raped
it was maury and mule
who managed to
open their mouth
and by turning into a donkey
changed his own
name and of things
the new mule learned
german and *vergewaltigung*
ceases to be what it is
becomes some sound
said with the same
intonation as comet
fury alligator bird
match procession stone
cactus

the packed mule
almost mute at least
never been deaf
‘i can even hear the stones and their misfortune’
each one has what the mule says
in zarathustra
hilst’s mule
but the nightingale who sings
is the male nightingale.

o meio-confesso

ao jogar lixo
no lixo e o lixo
não entrar no
lixo o que vale
não é a intenção
meia-confissão
há de voltar atrás
lidar com o lixo
pegar o lixo com a
mão terminar a
ação um lixo no
lixo não é lixo
o que faz o lixo
não é o cesto
o que faz o lixo
é o chão.

the half-confession

throwing trash
in the trash and the trash
not going into the
trash the intention
is not what counts
half-confession
will go back
deal with the trash
pick the trash up with the
hand finish the
deed some trash
in the trash is not trash
what makes it trash
is not the bin
what makes it trash
is the ground.

o envelope

adoro lamber envelope
eu gosto do gosto da cola
do envelope há algo
de devoção em lamber
papel e esse que
carrega o contrato
assinado com o advogado
leva dos fatos a minha versão
lambo esse envelope em pé
posto que esse papel lambido
é linguagem
e revolução.

the envelope

i love to lick the envelope
i like the taste of glue
on the envelope there is something
devout in licking
paper and this one that
carries the contract
signed with the lawyer
carries the facts of my own version
i lick this envelope while standing
as this licked piece of paper
is language
and revolution.

o cachorro

a mulher do grupo
de ajuda é boa como
um cão preciso encontrar
esteio e ela me conforta
adivinhando a primeira obsessão
não se avexar tudo
voltará ao normal
não acredito mas parece
fazer sentido se fizer
algum sentido que hoje
não dou como sei que
gosto e Humboldt fode
como fodem os
maridos.

the dog

the woman in the support
group is good like
a dog i need to find
solace she comforts me
guessing my first obsession
don't beat yourself up it
will all return to normal
i can't believe it but it seems
to make sense if it does
make sense that today
i don't put out the way i know
i like and Humboldt fucks
like husbands
do.

o elefante

quando johanna morreu tinha um ano
e oito meses foi encontrada na piscina
apertava um elefante na mão que sua mãe
até hoje aperta muito embora o alzheimer
lhe impeça de lembrar por que ela a mãe
pulou na piscina ao ver johanna
à deriva no ventinho do norte da renânia
boiando na piscina que o pai de johanna
esqueceu de cobrir enquanto jogava
tênis com outros amigos talvez tão ou mais
ricos do que eles a mãe de johanna que hoje
já não se lembra de muita coisa como falei
por causa do alzheimer lembrou no entanto
de guardar o elefante só esqueceu
de tirar o vestido molhado dizem que passou
dias assim 'parecia uma estátua grega' disseram
o que ninguém viu era que apertava também o
elefantinho em 1958 quando eu morri 50 anos
depois tinha vinte e cinco anos e seis meses e apertava
o primeiro verso de um poema de sylvia plath e resistia
bravamente de olhos fechados enquanto caía morto
o mundo inteiro embora soubesse que o resto do
poema é uma declaração de amor completamente idiota
como são todas as declarações de amor heterossexual
e como tantas coisas que plath escreveu recitava
o poema enquanto me afogava me perdoe plath me perdoe

the elephant

at the time of her death johanna was one year
and eight months old she was found in the pool
holding onto an elephant her mother
still holds today closely even though the alzheimer's
prevents her from remembering why she the mother
did not jump into the pool when she first saw johanna
drifting on the light northern rhineland wind
floating on the pool that johanna's father
forgot to cover as he played tennis
with his friends maybe as rich or more so
than themselves johanna's mother today
doesn't remember much like i said
because of the alzheimer's she did however remember
to keep the elephant only she forgot
to remove the wet dress they said she spent
days like that looking 'like a greek statue'
what no one noticed was that she held onto
the tiny elephant in 1958 when i died 50 years
later i was twenty-five years and six months old and i held onto
the first verse of a sylvia plath poem and resisted
fiercely with my eyes closed as the whole world
dropped dead even though i knew that the rest of the
poem is a declaration of love completely idiotic
as all declarations of heterosexual love are
so many things plath wrote i recited
the poem as i drowned forgive me plath forgive me

campilho o mundo é um horror o elefante é de pelúcia
e ossinhos não são de mel
são apenas cálcio
nada mais.

campilho the world is a horror the elephant is made of plush
and small bones are not made of honey
they are just calcium
nothing else.

para laura

em 1998 quando encontraram
o corpo gay de matthew shepard
sua cara tinha sangue por todo lado
menos duas listras
perpendiculares
que era por onde suas lágrimas
haviam escorrido
naquele dia o ciclista
que o encontrou não
ligou logo que o viu pra polícia
porque o corpo de matthew
estava tão deformado
que o ciclista achou ter visto
um espantalho

sábado passado em são paulo
um grupo de homens
e dois PMs mataram laura
não sem antes
torturá-la laura
foi vista ainda viva
por outro sujeito
que gravou
e postou no youtube o vídeo
de uma laura desorientada
e quem não estaria
com sangue jorrando da boca e da parte
de trás do vestido?

for laura

in 1998 when they found
the gay body of matthew shepard
his whole face was bloodied
but for two stripes
perpendicular
where his tears
had flowed
that day the cyclist
who found him did not
call the police immediately
because the body of matthew
was so disfigured
that the cyclist thought he'd seen
a scarecrow

last saturday in são paulo
a group of men
and two military police killed laura
not without first
torturing her laura
was seen still alive
by some guy
who recorded
and posted on youtube the video
of a laura disorientated
and who wouldn't be
blood spewing from the mouth and from the back
of the dress?

laura tem um corpo
e um nome que lhe pertencem
laura de vermont (presente!)
foi assassinada
por homens
pelo estado
e pela nossa indiferença
aos 18 anos
num sábado.

laura has a body
and a name that belong to her
laura de vermont (*presente*!)
was murdered
by men
by the state
and by our indifference
aged 18
on a saturday.

a visita

> and every bed has been condemned,
> not by morality or law,
> but by time
> – *Anne Sexton*

quais as traças
aranhas piolhos
e outras bestas
infestam habitam
o colchão de visitas
que Humboldt não foi buscar
fingindo esquecimento
depois foi tarde demais
e estávamos apaixonados
demais para buscar
o colchão de visitas
na água-furtada
então ficou por isso mesmo

quais as traças
aranhas piolhos
e outras bestas
em outro colchão
maldito testemunharam
outro colchão
outra visita
o arranque
o violento
o sangue

the visit

> and every bed has been condemned,
> not by morality or law,
> but by time
> – *Anne Sexton*

like the moths
spiders lice
and other beasts
infesting inhabiting
the guest mattress
which Humboldt did not pick up
pretending to forget
then it was too late
and we were in love
so much so that we did not pick up
the guest mattress
from the loft
and that was that

like the moths
spiders lice
and other beasts
in another damned
mattress witnessed
another mattress
another visit
the start
the violence
the blood

bom sangue não houve
houve a chegada
e depois silêncio
por areia teia pó
musgo mofo aranha
eu pulei para outra
cama outras bestas
antes já haviam me
habitado formigas
ácaros piscianos
percevejos só as
traças e Humboldt
não me comeram

anos antes a desdita
embora areia teia pó
musgo mofo aranha
não pude nunca mais
sair daquela cama
há bestas menos confiáveis
que traças há hienas
potós peixes serpentes
se há 2 no colchão
de 1 visita sempre
haverá um que não é
inocente.

well there was no blood
there was the arrival
and then the silence
through sand cobweb dust
moss mould spiders
i jumped into another
bed other beasts
before i had been
inhabited by ants
piscian mites
bedbugs only the
moths and Humboldt
did not bite me

years before the misfortune
even through sand cobwebs dust
moss mould spiders
i was never again
able to leave that bed
there are untrustworthy beasts
less so than moths there are hyenas
beetles fishes serpents
if there are 2 in the mattress
of 1 visitor there will always be one who is not
innocent.

a mulher casada

sento-me
em círculo
conforme
o evento
engulo
o vinho
deposito no
cantinho
caroços
de azeitonas
controlo
o período fértil
finjo-me
cadastrada
carteirinha
de vacinada
belo
animal doméstico
celebro
banalidades
participo
da conversa
volto pra casa
de carona
e muda
tenho na cabeça
coisinhas
sexo

the married woman

i sit in a circle
according
to the event
i swallow
the wine
i deposit
olive
pits on
the corner
i control
the fertile period
i pretend
to be registered
vaccinated
beautiful
domesticated animal
i celebrate
banalities
i engage
in conversation
i head home
get a lift
ride mute
in my mind
little things
sex
bikini
razors

biquíni
navalhas
viagens
as azeitonas
os guardanapos
os óvulos
canela amêndoa
ursos polares.

travel
the olives
the napkins
the eggs
cinnamon almond
polar bears.

o bom animal

quantos palmos
de largura tem
o seu quadril?
desconfio que
o meu seja
mais largo
ao menos
foi o que senti
ao sentar
em você
queria eu
ter sentado
na sua cara
gentil
como um bom animal
e submissa
como um bom animal
eu me alegraria
com sua língua em mim
e grata
como um bom animal
eu lamberia
sua cara
molhada
pegajosa
cheirando a mim
mas minha língua
minha pobre língua

the good animal

how many palms
wide is
your waist?
i suspect that
mine is
wider
at least
that's what i felt
when i sat
on you
i wish i
had sat
on your face
gentle
like a good animal
and submissive
like a good animal
i would cheer up
with your tongue in me
and grateful
like a good animal
i would lick
your face
wet
sticky
smelling of me
but my tongue
my poor tongue

só lambeu suas
pálpebras
Humbert Humboldt
eu não sou nenhuma
Henriette Herz
me deixe pousar
a cara em seu pau
e me afogar no
silêncio entre
suas coxas e testículos
sua magreza me insulta
Humboldt
mas para cada osso
Humboldt
me deixe lembrá-lo
há a carne
correspondente.

has only ever licked your
eyelids
Humbert Humboldt
i am no
Henriette Herz
let me land
my face on your cock
and drown in the
silence between
your thighs and testicles
your thinness insults me
Humboldt
but for each bone
Humboldt
let me remind you
there is flesh
corresponding.

o martelo

durmo com um martelo
embaixo do travesseiro
caso alguém entre de novo
e sorrateiro
no meu quarto não bastasse
ser um saco ter um ferro
me cutucando a cabeça
há ainda outro inconveniente:
Humboldt nunca pode chegar
de surpresa corre o risco
de ser martelado e assim
morrer ou viver
(a quantidade de energia
liberada pelo golpe de
um martelo
é equivalente à metade de
sua massa vezes a velocidade
ao quadrado na hora do impacto).

the hammer

i sleep with a hammer
under my pillow
in case someone walks in again
and as if sneaking
into my bedroom is not enough
being a pain and having an
iron poking me in the
head there's yet another inconvenience:
Humboldt may never come in
unannounced he runs the risk
of being hammered and thus
live or die
(the amount of energy
released by the blow of
a hammer
equals half its
mass times speed
squared at the time of impact).

Afterword

A hammer is a useful metaphor to have at the heart of your poetry collection. For protection, you can sleep with it under your pillow at night – according to both poems entitled 'the hammer' – or use it to drive a nail into the face of your enemy, Jael vs Sisera style, though the speaker of the second poem of that name insists: 'i never / hammered / anyone.' A hammer can be used to build things too. It's 'good for nailing a broadside to a wall' (Lotte Thießen, *artiCHOKE*) or for hitting metaphorical nails on the head during arguments – the final point made in the collection *o martelo* (here, the first poem in the selection). 'Being hammered' is synonymous with being drunk in both Portuguese and English and subconscious connections between getting hammered and having sex ('screwing' or 'getting nailed' in English) also perhaps lurk in the background.

The figurative link between hammers, judges and even popes and, with them, legal and religio-moral traditions that are not at all historically favourable to females or their testimonies, is, meanwhile, foregrounded. This is at its most explicit in 'the sentence' in which, following a rape trial brought by Ivánova's protagonist, she declares the *real* sentence behind a verdict that cannot tell 'the difference in the innocence / of the man and of the hyenas.' The judge brings down the hammer and, with it, the age-old conclusion that 'guilty is the woman': a sentence which 'weighs / weighs like an anvil' – the surface upon which a hammer strikes something – on the speaker's back. She, as an individual female, is symbolically an object caught beneath the blow of historically institutionalised misogyny. The judge's decree, we infer throughout the collection, is never the end of proceedings for the woman. As a final flourish, 'the sentence' includes a 'bequeath[ing]' of 'the trauma' which is always the survivor's weight to bear.

If the hammer of this poetry doubles as both tool of oppression as well as defense weapon of choice, this is apt, for uncanny doublings and leveled-out differences occur repeatedly in the poems. The original collection is split into two halves, in which two very different poems, both entitled 'the hammer', appear, one in each. The prince-antagonist is a recurring male figure and so is his opposite: the friend-lover-husband cipher that is Humboldt. But in one version of 'the hammer' and another poem, 'the visit', the ostensible origins of the speaker's love for Humboldt are saturated with slippages between Humboldt's visit and 'another mattress / another visit'. The latter poem ends with the observation that 'if there are 2 in the mattress / of 1 visitor there will always be one who is not / innocent.' Whether this is a reference to the sexual assault that occurred before the poetry begins – or of the speaker's implied infidelity somewhere in the gap between parts one and two? – is never made clear. Nor is it coincidental that the title of this poem, 'a visita', doubles as both 'visit' and 'visitor' in Portuguese. The other 'visitors' in this poem are 'beasts', such as lice, ants, mites and bedbugs, that infest and inhabit, i.e. enter the bed and even the body uninvited and unwanted. Though, sadly, these do not form part of the crowd of witnesses at the rape trial, according to another poem, and so cannot attest to the fact that, despite there being 'no blood [...] only silence', violence was still done.

The fact that it isn't always apparent who, or even what, is harming whom evokes the unresolved damage done to the speaker by the original assault: the traumatic event that remains unnamed and undescribed – like the speaker herself – at the centre of the poetry. The fraught condition of trying to reestablish the boundaries around one's identity and thought processes, of reclaiming the body and especially one's sexual desires, after experiencing such an assault, is communicated, instead, via repeated slippages between various, ostensibly conflicting states, such as lust / trauma, 'morality' / violence, despair / defiance – all of which are being grappled with within the context of the labyrinthine mechanics of the state at large.

For the unjust justice system experienced by Ivánova's speaker is another example of absurd doubling, in which the police are the criminals ('for laura'), and survivors of rape and other atrocities are forced (if they survive) to re-live, by re-telling, repeatedly, their original suffering, via the courts and other institutions, only to be disbelieved, like some fucked-up Nietszchean 'eternal return' of the same. In such an upended world, where guilt is declared to be innocence and vice versa, the speaker of 'the sentence' resorts, in anguish, to that which supposedly rendered her guilty in the first place:

> leave me alone!
>   rather fill me with wine
>
> the cup, even though awful might leave me
> drunk, console me the alcoholic amnesia
> and forget what is in fact the sentence:
>   guilty is the woman.
> [...]
>
> it's her fault: she stuffed her
>   drunken face.

If, according to Baudelaire's formulation, 'the horrible burden of time that breaks your back' is universal, and the only remedy for it is to 'be drunk!' there are still those – women, trans and gay people, for instance – who, like 'a mula', carry a double burden.

Moreover, we are reminded in Ivánova's work that such guilt-innocence and just-injustices, are as they have always been, according to a civil law system founded upon classical Roman law, added to in the late Middle Ages under the influence of canon or ecclesiastical law. For if, according to Christian doctrine, Eve is the original sinner, causing the fall of man and all our woe, the generalised guilt of womankind was shored up particularly colourfully throughout the Middle Ages by the early Church Fathers of Europe, who did much to disseminate the view that to be born a woman is to be born always already guilty, sexually insatiable, a temptress, more 'base' and 'animal' than man in every way.

These historical tropes are picked up by Ivánova. Note how often women are likened to or associated with animals in her work. Note, too, the presence of the mythic archetypes of women abused by and then silenced by men of power: 'tongueless Philomela', raped by her brother-in-law, her tongue cut out, so she could not report his crime, Lucretia, driven to suicide from the shame of having been raped, and Lavinia, from Shakespeare's *Titus Andronicus*, raped and mutilated: her arms, as well as tongue, cut off by her attackers, finally murdered by her own father: 'Because the girl should not survive her shame, / And by her presence still renew his sorrows.' Constantine the Great, first Christian Emperor of Rome, would have approved of this action. He it was who decreed a law proclaiming *raptus* to be a case of theft against the property of the head of the household – the father. If the female consented to her own abdication or elopement, without his permission, she would be burnt alive along with her male 'abductor'. If she had not consented, she was still punished, 'on the grounds that she could have saved herself by screaming for help.'

We could discuss similarly contradictory injustices perpetuated by state-church and church-state in the context of so many parts of the world right now:

> in pakistan if the victim
> is unable to find four eye
> witnesses she is the one being
> prosecuted ('the testicles')

To say nothing of the 'developed' world's current concerted attack on women's hard-fought rights. But to concentrate on Catholic Brazil, where Ivánova grew up, religious law and state law have been especially historically entangled, and women (cis and trans), and gay people, the poetry reminds us, have always fared badly at the hands of laws bequeathed to man from 'a misogynous god', according to another poem by Ivánova.

In fact, in this collection, nothing is easily disentangled from anything else, and that is the point. As Humboldt's namesake, Alexander von, suggested centuries ago: 'everything is interconnected.' The experience of gendered violence carries after-effects, the damage from which the protagonist is still negotiating and internalising ('the dog') in every succeeding relationship. The same slave-owning patriarchy descended from 'greek man-thology', according to another poem, where only noblemen counted as the demos, the people, is precursor to the law in eighteenth century England whereby, we are told, if a rape victim had 'not screamed and resisted / it would be established that the complaint was invalid'.

The non-sequential narrative of the poems, in which there is no clear progression of events from one poem to the next, or indeed within each poem, is an effective and affective rendering of 1. the fact that history seems to repeat itself and 2. the disorienting nature of the violences depicted – their dizzying aftereffects and attendant flashbacks. Ivánova also maximises poetic techniques such as a lack of expected punctuation, that would provide clear footholds of grammatical sense, and the resulting ambivalences, zeugma, parataxis, enjambic non sequiturs, as well as neologisms (composite words) and tautological repetition, to draw equivalences between unlike things and create a sense of no sense, or what 'returning to normal' might look like, post-trauma, in a world of recurring injustice: 'i can't believe it but it seems / to make sense if it does / make sense' ('the dog').

At times, the usual literary 'contract' between a simile and what it represents is broken; for instance, the first two stanzas of 'the visit' both begin with the word 'like' which is left free-floating. At other times, where we are set up to expect explanation, we get only vertiginous lists:

years before the misfortune
although sand cobwebs dust
moss mould spiders

How could a language construction, the conjunction 'although', qualify / explain / denote something as world-altering as sexual assault anyway? the poetry seems to be asking us. And how could a testimony, mere sequence of signifiers, ever balance in the scales against such an act of violence (the signified), when words are that which equalise and flatten, language being a chain of sign-sounds that are 'arbitrary and differential' (Ferdinand de Saussure):

and *vergewaltigung*
ceases to be what it is
becomes some sound
said with the same
intonation as comet
fury alligator bird
match procession stone
cactus. ('the mule')

These are rhetorical questions, since there is always the difference of intention and that is everything. It is, for instance, the difference between consensual and non-consensual sex, despite a rape culture's apparent difficulty recognising it: 'and if they think of / rape as sex it's because they have /no idea (like i do) of what / a good fuck is' ('the testicles').

If language's deficiencies are always apt for misconstruction, Ivánova's poetry foregrounds these dangers and makes of them a strength. In her poems the argument for fragmentation, over coherent 'story', is proposed; the pleasure, as well as the necessity of its extremities, and the illuminations it can bring. That which catches the eye as a result of a break may be buried in normative discourse, just as a window pane is transparent until broken – smashed with a hammer? – each piece glinting separately with reflected light. Humboldt too – like the German

Romantics before him – may have held that the fragment is our only access to the whole.

Against the 'grand narratives' we still tell 'to justify a single set of laws and stakes [that] are inherently unjust', foregrounded by Jean-François Lyotard so many decades ago, Ivánova gives us these 'little' testimonies: poems which refuse to relinquish 'the facts of my own version' ('the envelope'). Against the centuries-old attempts of church, mosque or state to control, obsessively, the bodies of women, and guard against their impurity, the poems make exhilarating, sacrilegious turns. Take for instance, the speaker's love of licking the envelope (in the poem of that name), its taste of glue: 'there is something / devout in licking', she says, in an image that is part sexual metaphor, part transubstantiated wafer, except that she *isn't* kneeling:

> as this licked piece of paper
> is language
> and revolution. ('the envelope')

Against forgetting, silence and our collective 'indifference', we are given the tender memorials of a number of real human beings, killed by the state of things as they are and should not be. Yet, against the pull of so much despair, Ivánova does playfulness, humour, and, most importantly, fighting back.

Philomela fought back, Lavinia fought back. Note all the other women who show up in this writing: Ingeborg Bachmann, Sylvia Plath, Anne Sexton, Adília Lopes, Emily Dickinson, Matilde Campilho, Hilda Hilst, Anna Swirzcynska. The alternative to women not speaking back or out, the muteness of patriarchal socialisation (see 'the married woman' or 'the mule') is perhaps to be feared most of all. Ivánova reminds us that, against oppression, there will always be resistance, however manifested: testimony woven into a tapestry, or written in the sand with a stick, or even poetry.

Emily Critchley

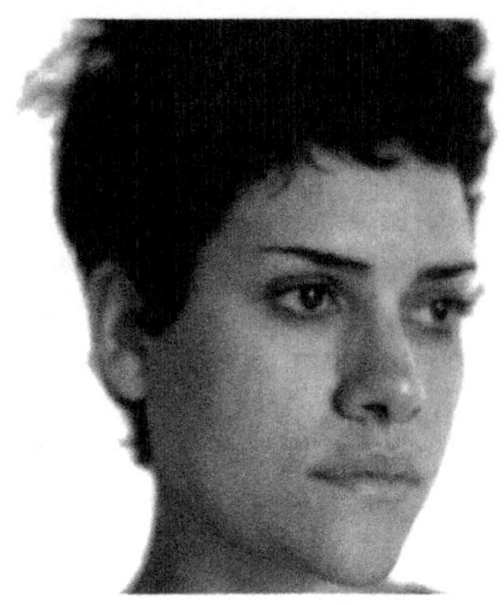

Adelaide Ivánova is a journalist and political activist whose practice includes poetry, photography, performance, translation and publishing. Her poems have been translated into English, Galician, German, Greek, Italian and Spanish. Her work has appeared in *The Huffington Post* (USA), *Marie Claire* (BR), *clinic* (UK), *alba londres* (UK), *Lateinamerika Nachrichten* (GER), *artiCHOKE* (GER), *Modern Poetry in Translation* (UK). Her photographic work is part of the collection of Kunst Museum Dieselkraftwerk (Germany), L'arthotèque – Museum of Fine Arts (France) and the Galeria Murilo Castro (Brazil). She edits the anarco-feminist zine *MAIS PORNÔ, PVFR!* and is co-founder of RESPEITA!, a coalition of Brazilian female poets and spoken-word artists. She lives in Berlin, where she tries to earn a living as a babysitter, life model, waiter and other alienating jobs.

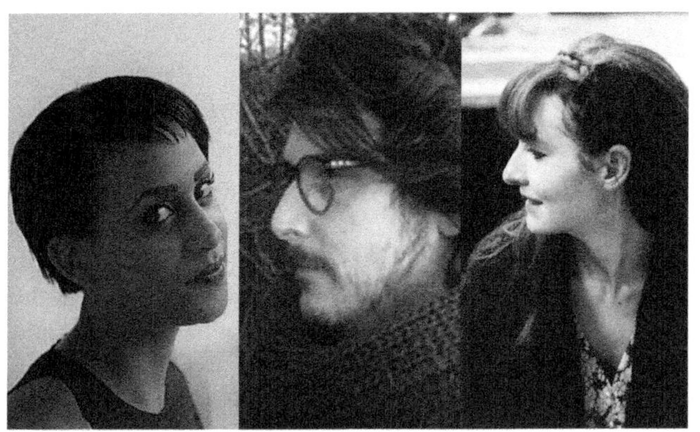

Rachel Long is a poet & the founder of Octavia – Poetry Collective for Womxn of Colour. Octavia was founded in response to the lack of inclusivity and representation in poetry and the academy. Her work has featured in *Magma*, *The London Magazine*, and *Filigree: An Anthology of Contemporary Black British Poetry*. She is co-tutor on the Barbican Young Poets Programme and Poetry Fellow of University of Hertfordshire.

Francisco Vilhena is assistant editor at *Granta* magazine. He writes short essays and translates from the Portuguese; his work can be found in *Modern Poetry in Translation*, *clinic*, *Wasafiri*, *Brooklyn Rail*, *Granta* and elsewhere. He has served as bridge translator on several PTC translation workshops. His cat is one of the first feline polyglots.

Emily Critchley is the author of several poetry collections, including *Arrangements* (Shearsman, 2018), *Ten Thousand Things* (Boiler House, 2017) and a selected writing: *Love / All That / & OK* (Penned in the Margins, 2011). She is editor of *Out of Everywhere 2: Linguistically Innovative Poetry by Women in North America & the UK* (Reality Street, 2016) and is Senior Lecturer in English and Creative Writing at the University of Greenwich.

About the Poetry Translation Centre

Set up in 2004, the Poetry Translation Centre is the only UK organisation dedicated to translating, publishing and promoting contemporary poetry from Africa, Asia and Latin America. We introduce extraordinary poets from around the world to new audiences through books, online resources and bilingual events. We champion diversity and representation in the arts, and forge enduring relations with diaspora communities in the UK. We explore the craft of translation through our long-running programme of workshops which are open to all.

The Poetry Translation Centre is based in London and is an Arts Council National Portfolio organisation. To find out more about us, including how you can support our work, please visit: www.poetrytranslation.org.

About the World Poet Series

The World Poet Series offers an introduction to some of the world's most exciting contemporary poets in an elegant pocket-sized format. The books are presented as bilingual editions, with the English and original-language text displayed side by side. The translations themselves have emerged from specially commissioned collaborations between leading English-language poets and bridge-translators. Completing each book is an afterword essay by a UK-based poet, responding to and contextualising the work for the reader.